D0788861

This book belongs to…

_____

_____

FREE Monthly Stories & Dances Workshop

JOIN our Facebook Group "Raise Multicultural Kids" for details

www.CultureGroove.com/Free

Pronunciation Guide

Bhaiya – Bhuh–ee–aa

Chandni – Chaand–nee

Delhi – Del–lee

Jahan – Juh–haan

Jalebi – Juh–lay–bee

Jantar Mantar – Jun–tur Mun–tur

Kohinoor – Koh–hee–noor

Kila – Kee–laa

Minar – Mee–naar

Mumtaz – Moom–taaz

Qutub – Koo–tube

Samrat – Some–raat

Taj Mahal – Taaj Mahal

Vishal – Vee–shaal

Note for parents: Our books provide a glimpse into the beautiful cultural diversity of India, including occasional mythology references. In this book, we showcase elements of Delhi and Taj Mahal that are best suited for young readers to follow.

Copyright © 2016, 2017, 2018 by Bollywood Groove™, Culture Groove. All rights reserved. This book or any portion thereof may not be reproduced or used in any manner whatsoever without the express written permission of the publisher except for the use of brief quotations in a book review.
Printed in the United States of America. First Edition.

Maya & Neel's India Adventure Series, Book 10

Let's Visit
Delhi & Taj Mahal!

Raise Multicultural Kids

Written by:
Ajanta & Vivek

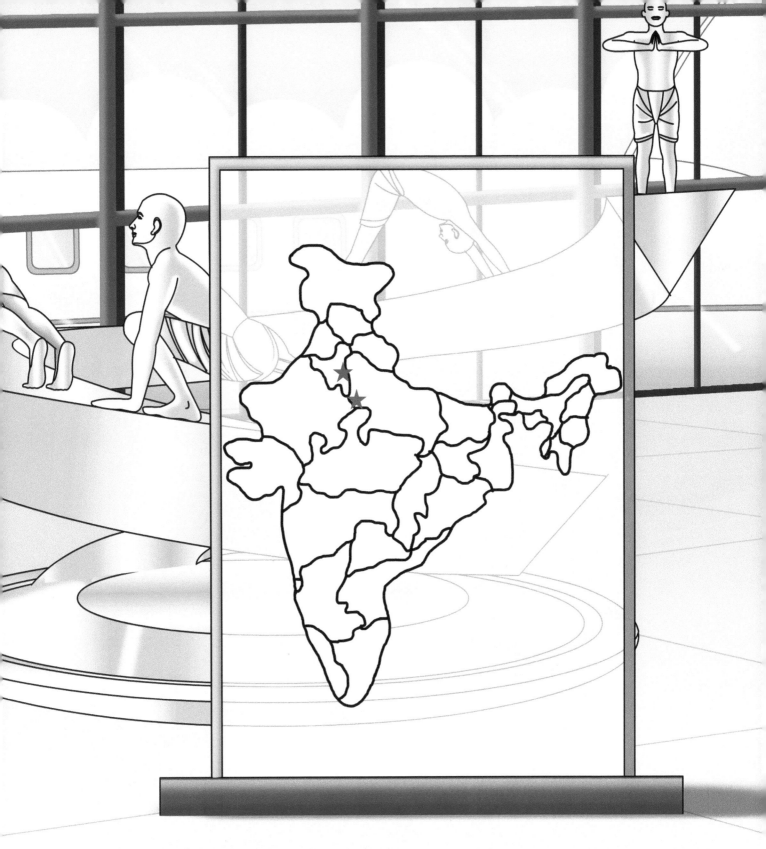

This is a map of India. India is a big country. It has many states, languages, festivals, and dances.

Do you see the blue star on the map? That is where Delhi is.

Do you see the red star? That is where Taj Mahal is.

Maya, Neel & Chintu arrive at their cousin Vishal's house. In Hindi, brother is called *Bhaiya*.

"Vishal *Bhaiya*, we are so excited to explore Delhi with you," Maya says. "Yes, we will have a fun adventure!" Vishal smiles. He gives them warm hugs.

"Come inside and rest," Vishal brings them in, "Tomorrow we will visit a very cool building called the Red Fort."

They head out early next morning and reach a massive red building. "This is *Laal Kila*. It means Red Fort. A long time ago, kings and queens lived here" Vishal says.

Maya and Neel stare in wonder. They have never seen such a big fort.

"Who made this fort, Vishal *Bhaiya*?" Neel asks. "A king named Shah Jahan" Vishal replies while showing them around.

"This fort used to have the world's largest diamond. It's called the Kohinoor diamond," Vishal adds.

Neel closes his eyes to imagine a massive sparkly stone. "It must have been so cool," he says dreamily.

"Let's go, kids," Vishal laughs. "I want to show you an exciting evening concert."

Later in the evening, they arrive in front of a huge stage with bright lights. They see dancers and musicians on stage. Maya & Neel love the music and dance along.

"This concert is called the *Qutub* festival. Do you see that tall building behind the stage? That is the tallest brick building in the world. It is called *Qutub Minar*," Vishal explains.

"How tall is it?" Neel asks.

"Hmmm" Vishal thinks, "If about 75 4-year-olds stood on each other's shoulders, they will finally reach the top."

The next morning, the kids wake up very excited.

Vishal had mentioned last night about riding a rickshaw.

Maya, Neel and Chintu cannot wait to find out what that is.

They arrive at a very busy place. The streets are filled with people, cars, motorcycles and cool looking bike rides called rickshaws.

They climb onto a rickshaw and the driver paddles along. "Kids, this place is called *Chandni Chowk*. It is a big market," Vishal shares.

After a fun rickshaw ride, Vishal takes them to a food shop. A man is squeezing a cloth filled with gooey white dough. The dough drops into hot oil and comes out in fun round shapes.

"Wow, this smells amazing!" Maya and Neel sniff. Chintu nods.

"This is called *Jalebi*" Vishal explains. The kids and Chintu bite into the sweet, crunchy *Jalebi* and look very happy.

The next morning, they drive up to a place with very cool looking structures. Maya and Neel cannot tell what these structures are.

"This is *Jantar Mantar*," Vishal says with a wide sweep of his hand.

"These structures were made to measure how the sun, moon and planets move around in space," Vishal adds.

"What is that triangle-shaped one?" Maya points to a tall structure.

"Ah, that is a sun dial. Let me tell you more." Vishal says.

Sun dial at Jantar Mantar

This triangle-shaped structure at Jantar Mantar is called *Samrat Yantra* or the King's Instrument. It is a sundial and a giant clock.

A sundial works by measuring the position of the sun's shadow. *Samrat Yantra* is a clock that can tell time very correctly. You can even make a sun dial yourself.

Make your own sundial

What you need:

Paper plate

Pencil

Ruler

Straw

How to make

1. Write the number 12 on one corner of the plate. Draw a line from the center of the plate to number 12.

2. Stick a straw through the center of the plate

3. Bring the plate outside at noon and set it on the ground. Make sure the shadow of the straw falls exactly on the line from the center to 12.

4. After every hour, mark the position of the shadow by writing 1, 2, 3 and so on.

5. The next day, you can tell what time it is by looking where the shadow falls.

Early next morning, they all get in a car for a long drive.

On the way, they see a massive gate.

"This is the famous India Gate," Vishal explains "India Gate was made to remember brave soldiers".

The kids look out the window quietly and enjoy the beautiful scene.

They drive for a long time and take a snack break.

"We are now in a place called Agra," Vishal says.

Neel spots a big white building in the distance. "What is that building with a dome? It looks magical," Neel asks.

"That is the world famous Taj Mahal," Vishal smiles.

His eyes sparkle with excitement.

"I bet you have never seen anything like it," he says with a mysterious smile. Chintu jumps up and down.

All four of them walk up to the Taj Mahal. Their jaws drop and they stare in wonder. Taj Mahal is even more beautiful up close.

"It is sparkly white like a magical palace," Maya exclaims. Chintu claps his hands. "Let me tell you more about Taj Mahal," Vishal says.

Story of Taj Mahal

Once there was a king named Shah Jahan.

He had a queen named Mumtaz Mahal.

The king and queen loved each other very much.

Sadly, Mumtaz Mahal died. Shah Jahan was very sad. He decided to build the Taj Mahal to remember her.

It took 20 years to make the Taj Mahal.

Do you know 1000 elephants helped to make the Taj Mahal? Elephants are very strong. They can carry heavy things.

Taj Mahal means Crown of Palace. It is made out of white marble.

Where else have you seen marble? Kitchen counters maybe?

It took 20,000 people to make the Taj Mahal. That is a lot of people!

If you spoke to each person for 1 minute, you will have to talk non-stop for 14 days and nights.

"Wow! That was one amazing adventure," Maya says.

"Yes, we learned so much about Delhi and the Taj Mahal. This is now one of our favorite cities to visit," Neel says.

Chintu nods. He does a happy squirrel dance.

"We cannot wait for our next adventure. I wonder where that will be. We hope you can join us then!" Maya, Neel, and Chintu say.

"Until then, Namaste!"

Let's look back on our wonderful trip to Delhi & Taj Mahal

What does *Laal Kila* mean?
Red Fort

What is the tallest brick building in the world?
Qutub Minar

Why did they make India Gate?
To remember brave soldiers

What is the sun dial at Jantar Mantar called?
Samrat Yantra

What is the famous building in Agra called? *Taj Mahal*

Where did they take a
rickshaw ride?
Chandni Chowk

What dessert did they
eat in Chandni Chowk?
Jalebi

What is a sun dial?
A giant clock

Which animals helped in
making Taj Mahal?
Elephants

What is Taj
Mahal made of?
Marble

About the Authors

Ajanta Chakraborty was born in Bhopal, India, and moved to North America in 2001. She earned an MS in Computer Science from the University of British Columbia and also earned a Senior Diploma in Bharatanatyam, a classical Indian dance, to feed her spirit.

Ajanta quit her corporate consulting job in 2011 and took the plunge to run Bollywood Groove (and also Culture Groove) full-time. The best part of her work day includes grooving with classes of children as they leap and swing and twirl to a Bollywood beat.

Vivek Kumar was born in Mumbai, India, and moved to the US in 1998. Vivek has an MS in Electrical Engineering from The University of Texas, Austin, and an MBA from the Kellogg School of Management, Northwestern University.

Vivek has a very serious day job in management consulting. But he'd love to spend his days leaping and swinging, too.

We have been featured on:

We are independent authors who want to help **Raise Multicultural Kids**! We rely on your support to sustain our work:

- ✓ Drop us an Amazon review at: **CultureGroove.com/books**

- ✓ **Share our books as Gifts & Party Favors** (bulk order discounts)

- ✓ Schedule our unique **'Dancing Bookworms' Virtual Author Visits**

- ✓ Join our **FREE** Monthly Stories & Dances workshops: **CultureGroove.com/FREE**

Many thanks!

Culture Groove
Raise Multicultural Kids

CPSIA information can be obtained
at www.ICGtesting.com
Printed in the USA
BVHW021009120722
641924BV00010B/758